Mindful Horseback Riding

Alecz Adams

Published by Alecz Adams and Russell Granger, 2023.

Table of Contents

.... 1

I. Introduction 6

II. Mindfulness 10

Box Breathing 12

The Healing Horseshoe 13

III. Mindful Groundwork 19

In Hand 20

Grooming 21

Bending 24

Respecting Direction 25

Unwinding 28

Lunging 29

Using the lunge whip 30

Lunging Formation 31

Speeding Up 33

Slowing Down 34

Turns 36

Come 'ere 37

Starting the Lunge Circle 38

Alleviating Dizziness 40

Breathing With Steps From A Distance 41

Mindful Walking 43

Trustwork 45

Go 47

Turn 49

Stop 52

Connecting 54

More Advanced 56

IV. Mindful Horseback Riding 58

Dismounted Stretches 59

Yoga on Horseback 61

Basic Position 62

Arms Shoulder Height 66

Bends and Turns 67

Chest Opening 69

Triangle 70

Mounted Walking Meditation 71

Circle 73

Figure Eight 75

Transitions 76

Higher Ground 79

Sitting Trot 81

Posting Trot 83

Cantering or Loping 85

Getting Perspective 87

V. Conclusion 90

Mindful Horseback Riding

by Alecz Adams

MINDFUL HORSEBACK RIDING

Copyright @ 2019 by Alecz Adams

This book is dedicated to all

the equines who teach us and love us.

May we always be worthy of you.

Acknowledgements

Bob Overstreet, for absolutely everything. This particular time, for your hand in bringing this book to manifest.

Funny Zofcin, for all the hours you gave to the outdoor world, and chores, and everything else, so that I could complete this book.

Russell Granger, for your editing, modeling, friendship, and overall goodness.

Sara Divya for her unwavering belief, Mary Kate Jordan for love and advice, Bonsai, Kath Rossi because you are the motivation behind the very first written copy of the Healing Horseshoe Meditation, MVHR, Jenny McCarthy, Mary Wolf, Sienna LaRene, Mark Gelinas, Lance Secretan, Claire Fox, Isa Gucciardi, Dave Kelly, The Weiss Family, Devins' Family.

My human models and photographers (and for some, so much more!): Emalea Landgraf, Vanda Whittaker, Linda Quiring, Julia Denault Parker, Joanne Kelley, Maddie Fetterolf, Noah Starling, Becky Green, Lynn Davis, Samantha "Irish" Baskin, Tamra Converse, Stewart Greisman, Barb Siray, David Sandberg, Brian Patty, Stacey Angst, Andrew Lecy, Kathryn Galer, Linda Pankuch, Dina Hampa, Joshua Beauford, Lily Hair, Karla Kerekes, Cathy Zeeb, Russell Granger, Cliff Keen, Leila and Shana Devins, Nellie Bradford, Nancy Knight, Steve Stennes

And most importantly, my marvelous equine models: Montana, Mariah, Latigo, Boone, Gabi, Be, Santi, Karma, Bonnie, Marty, Merlin, Journey, Kizzy, Robbie, Sparky, Stormy, Racey, Dot, Reba, Rodeo, Breezie, Atir, Thunder, April, Leo, Convict, Union, Chance (the dog)

I. Introduction

I wanted to write a book that would help interested horse enthusiasts come to a deeper understanding of their horses and other animals friends. I have always felt that effective communication and mutual understanding are truly integral to safety and enjoyment, no matter what endeavor one is discussing.

In these pages, I offer the techniques, tools, and methods which I have been developing and using with horse and human students for decades, in both North and South America. They are really very simple, and my wish is that this book will enhance your connection with your horse in some way. You may find similarities between my methods and those of others. That may be because many of these techniques just are simply Great Truths, and since they work, many great horse people have discovered them in their own ways, throughout time. I feel that much of the time, what differentiates those of us who choose to share knowledge with others is our means of conveying information. If I can help one person who wouldn't otherwise understand these concepts and practices to be able to do so, that's the most wonderful thing in the world. And anybody could be that person who changes everything. If my contribution to the equine world can help make a difference in the life of 1 horse, or 1 person… then I have succeeded.

I have spent a large part of my life with horses, as a competitor, a horse trainer, a riding instructor and an Equine Assisted Therapy and Therapeutic Riding provider. I find my passion with horses in interpreting horses for their humans, and then teaching their humans how to understand their horses themselves. I do a lot of work with horse rescues and rescue horses, probably because I, myself, have always rooted for the underdog. Someone gave up on every horse that becomes a rescue. I find joy in turning horses like that around and finding them forever homes, and many times, these mindful techniques are the breakthrough methods that bring a disheartened horse (or human) to the acceptance of love and a renewed outlook on life.

Some of these methods I use in my Equine Assisted Therapy programs, with great success, as they translate over easily to pets in the home. I highly recommend applying these techniques where ever they seem to fit into your world - with your household pets and barnyard animals, and even with your friends and family. People even report experiences like improvement in their golf game when applying practices from this book to other aspects of their daily life.

II. Mindfulness

The idea of establishing a deep connection between a horse and its rider is not a new concept. Fine-tuning that connection has been pursued all around the world. From the finest Spanish and Austrian riding schools to India's horse yogis and the innumerable indigenous people who have developed very unique and connected relationships with not only horses, but all kinds of animals, worldwide.

Mindfulness, in very simplified terms, is meditating in motion, and one might say that it is very much the practice of being present. Being present means thinking only about what is happening at this very moment, not allowing your mind to try to multi-task, to wander, day dream, or focus anywhere other than right where you are at that very moment. Not planning for the future and not assessing the past. Horses are a phenomenal conduit for this practice, as they themselves, as animals – and particularly prey animals – are so much more present in their daily experience of existence than humans are. When we humans can focus our exemplary observation skills on just what is happening with the horse and its environment, we can learn a lot. First, one must quiet the incessant chatter that occupies space in most of our own minds.

Perhaps you are somewhat new to the idea of mindfulness, but you are interested in a deeper connection with your horse. One of my favorite descriptions of mindfulness comes from the Buddhist poet Thict Naht Hahn. To summarize, in my own words: ... Think of how a cloud is formed. It draws water up from the oceans and rivers and creeks, into the sky. It all collects there, and when enough moisture collects, then it rains. It rains down water, and we gather that water and we put it into our kettle, and we boil it. Then we pour it over the leaves in our cup, which makes tea. So, as we look into our cup of tea, when we are mindful, we can see the clouds.

Mindfulness serves us in our work with horses by helping us to stay focused on, and subsequently respectful to, our equine friends. When you are mindful, you see not only the horse walking, or trotting, but you notice where the horse is carrying their head; how they're holding their tail; the length of the strides they are making: After enough practice, if you can't already, you will be able to tell your horse's mood, and how that changes with your actions and the activities you do with them. Trainers and very experienced horse people are often completely unaware that they themselves are using these exact methods to assess their horses each and every moment. However no matter how good you already are, you can improve your horsemanship skills just by being mindful... or more mindful.

Box Breathing

You can begin to practice mindfulness by quieting your mind. The first place I normally start introducing people to mindfulness practices is through breathwork. If you are not familiar with it, breathwork is simply counting combined with breathing and holding your breath. That's it. For instance, there is Box Breathing. That is just a name that describes the action of the breathwork practice itself. In Box Breathing you breathe in to a count of four, you hold for a count of four, you exhale to a count of four, and then you hold the out breath for a count of four, and you repeat that whole pattern 4 times. When I count it for people, it goes like this:

In 2, 3, 4... hold 2, 3, 4...out 2, 3, 4 ...hold the out breath 2, 3, 4. In 2, 3, 4... hold 2, 3, 4...out 2, 3, 4 ...hold the out breath 2, 3, 4. In 2, 3, 4... hold 2, 3, 4...out 2, 3, 4 ...hold 2, 3, 4. Last one in 2, 3, 4... hold 2, 3, 4...out 2, 3, 4 ...hold 2, 3, 4, return to normal breathing.

Try it. Right now. Chances are, you'll feel calmer and more relaxed, after just 64 seconds.

Part of the reason regulated breathing works, scientifically, has to do with oxygenation of the bloodstream. Think about how you breathe when you are upset, or stressed, or even really focused. We say we "forget to breathe" sometimes, but really, in these circumstances, we are generally breathing so shallowly that we just aren't doing an efficient job of getting enough air into our blood to feed the parts of our bodies that need it. When we do not breathe deeply enough, we are actually suffocating our brains. In addition, it is starving our muscles, because having enough oxygen in our blood is how we get oxygen to the rest of our bodies, including our brains. When we are mindful, and use breathing as a tool to our advantage, we truly and effectively set ourselves – and our horses – up for success.

The Healing Horseshoe

Another practice that can be expansive and enjoyable is using a horse as a focal point in a guided meditation. The Healing Horseshoe, below, is a visualization practice that I created. I do this with groups that can be very large, even into the hundreds. You may want to read then remember this and try it with your horse; or you can read the following into a recorder, like your cell phone, and play it back while you are with your horse; or you might have someone read it aloud to you as you paint the pictures in your mind with your horse.

This practice is similar to a guided visualization, but by incorporating the actual environment, including your horse, we create a slightly different experience.

Begin by facing your horse. If you want to relax and focus in your house or office, you can close your eyes and just picture your horse. If you are with your horse, I recommend at least the first time or two you try this, be just a little ways off from your horse, perhaps they are tied or behind a fence. This is so you can continue to focus on the meditation without having to worry about correcting your horse, or getting pushed over as he wanders over to see why you're there.

As you go through the meditation, if you are with your horse, begin by looking at all the unique details that make up your horse. Their manes and the hairs on the tips of their tails, their hocks, their fetlocks... their eyelashes, the hairs inside their ears, the hairs around their coronet bands just above their hooves, the hairs at their docks as their backs turn into their tails...take in every tiny detail of the horse you are looking at, and then close your eyes and picture that horse in your mind. Use your imagination to paint all those details there. Then after a moment, open your eyes and compare your vision of the horse with the reality of the horse. There is no wrong, there is only observing. Repeat this generally once or twice before continuing. If you are not physically with the horse you are picturing, just picture it in your mind. If you find this very difficult, I suggest getting a picture of the horse and using the attention to detail practice while looking at the photo.

Do your best to picture your horse in your mind, and if you are physically with your horse, there are several ways you may feel most comfortable proceeding. You can close your eyes for the experience. If you do, you may want to look at your horse from time to time throughout the practice. Also, if you choose to close your eyes, be sure that if you are standing, that you do not lock your knees. Locking your knees can result in falling over. If you want to stand with your eyes closed, but don't feel quite secure in your balance, you can keep your eyes closed, but periodically open your eyelids just a quarter of the way, regain your composure, and then gently shut them again. Repeat this as often as you feel necessary. You can also lean against something, or put your hand on something to help you balance remain in balance more. If you choose, you could always sit, but I do not suggest sitting in a location where your horse may push you over or step on you, or in a location you could get too relaxed and fall off, like a fence or something similar. And of course, you can always do the practice with your eyes open, ideally staring right at the horse you are working with. With an excellent imagination, you should have no trouble at all with any of the visualizations, even with your eyes open.

As you find yourself getting comfortable, begin to allow yourself to consider the idea that as you breathe in, you can actually bring in some of the energy that surrounds you, like relaxation or confidence, or similar positive feelings that you can imagine are just floating around you all of the time.

Now just begin to notice the surface that you are on. Notice all the places that this surface meets the different parts of your body. Your head, your back, your arms, your legs, your feet. And then just beginning to notice your breathing. Noticing where your breath goes as you breath in, and where your breath goes as you breathe out. You may notice your breath as it goes past the hairs in your nose, or on your upper lip, or you may notice it in the rise and fall of your belly, or your chest.

As you are aware of your breath in this way, just begin to notice the positive aspects of your surroundings. If it is quiet, you might recognize that as relaxation. If it is noisy, you could choose to perceive that as energy. If it is windy or cool, this could be felt as invigorating. And if it is sunny, you could notice how that feels like the warmth of love. Find something positive in your experience of your environment, and breathe it in.

Also, breathe that confidence, and kindness, and strength of your horse in, and, using your breath, allow all those positive parts of this horse and your surroundings to fill up your head and face. Just letting the inner corners of your eyes relax back into your head, while letting the outer corners of your eyes relax widely back towards your ears. With each breath you take in, allow all this positivity to fill your neck and throat. Using your breath, imagine filling up your arms, and chest, and belly. And just imagining that all of your organs in your chest and belly are now all bathed in a joyous, gentle, relaxation.

Continuing to use your breath to bring in all those positive aspects of your surroundings, and of your horse, and filling yourself completely, filling your legs all the way down to your feet. Now just noticing how your whole body, even the whole back of your body, is now filled with relaxation, and peace, and all of those other positive aspects of your surroundings, including all the positive aspects of your horse. You may notice that you feel so filled up with all these good feelings that they are spilling out of the pores of your body, and encircling you in a cloud, or surrounding you in cocoon of soothing, gentle energy.

Now as you feel yourself supported in this way, turn your attention again to your horse. You can open your eyes and look at your horse again, then you can either choose to close your eyes again or leave them open. See your horse, look at the details of your horse, and notice the way the light is hitting your horse. Now see, visualize, or imagine that the light you can differentiate in your horse's coat isn't actually from an external source, but is really emanating from within your horse.

See a ball of white or golden light, which appears as though it is light from the sun or a star, that is actually becoming apparent as the source of the light that you see in your horse's coat, radiating out from within. As you continue to visualize, watch that light growing brighter, and expanding within your horse, filling its neck and hindquarters, its head, and tail, and ears, and all the way down into all four legs, and hooves. Then, I wonder if you can imagine that light has begun to fill up the ground your horse is standing on. Visualize that light expanding out and forming a column of light, that at first surrounds just your horse, and then begins reaching deeper down, into the earth, and begins to stretch up into the sky, and continues to keep expanding to encompass you, and the general area, and perhaps your whole ranch, and community. The column of light just keeps expanding out and out, up and up, until it rains down all that light and love all over every place and every person and animal in the area, sharing all that light, and making you, and your horse, feel absolutely relaxed, empowered, and ready for whatever may come next.

When I do this for a private group – like a Girl Scout Troop, or a bank doing a team building class – at the close of this mindful meditation, I always ask everyone to give me a word to describe how they feel after doing this. Even if you are doing this practice by yourself, stop at the close of it, and reflect for a moment about how you feel after doing this practice, and find a word.

I want to include one more technique here, for helping to clear your mind of thoughts that are unnecessary while you are working with your horse in this way. For just a moment, take the time to notice your thoughts. Noting what is happening around you is just fine. Noticing the way your wrist moves as you use the body brush on your horse, the rhythm of your horse's breaths, the plane going by overhead. Noticing is fine, but when you find yourself thinking about those things stop, and let that go. It's fine to notice the plane, but if you notice your brain is attaching to having heard the plane, which you would notice by thoughts suddenly coming into your head like: "I wonder what kind of plane that is? I wonder where they are going? I need to take a trip! Where do I want to go...?" This is the time to practice letting your thoughts go, because obviously, taking a plane ride on vacation somewhere is not related to your time with your horse right now. Notice thoughts like that coming into your head, look at them, identify them as "thinking", and then just let them go, to drift down and away, return your attention for a moment to your breathing, the way it feels as your breath goes in and out, then return to your mindful practice with your horse.

This chapter has been meant to introduce people in search of mindful experiences with horses to just a few very basic techniques which will help you to begin the practice of being mindful with your horse.

III. Mindful Groundwork

As with any training program, groundwork is paramount as you begin. As our goal is Mindful Horseback Riding, we will include a few different steps, which we inclusively refer to as Mindful Groundwork. I am going to state here that, for the sake of this book, I will assume that you have a somewhat trained horse. A horse that is not overly dangerous, and at least fairly predictable. Although as a trainer, I do much work addressing equine behavioral complaints, this book is about connecting in a different way.

I would also like to mention as we begin here in groundwork, the amazing training and assimilation technique that is: The Pause. I cannot express how valuable this mindful practice may be in your work with horses. After each task, stop, take a breath, and Pause. Once your horse is walking or trotting, and has just returned to the rail after executing a movement, Pause, which may just mean allowing your horse to continue along without direction for a breath or two. Connect different movements, like trotting and turning, more quickly and expertly as you master each level of difficulty, but in the meantime, Pause.

In Hand

Being mindful in working with horses comes in many forms. Asking a horse to give you its trust can be the same. Begin as you approach your horse in their environment. Be mindful of your horse and the vicinity. How are they standing, facing you or facing away? Are there other horses nearby, or is your horse alone? Do they appear restless, relaxed, concerned, or lethargic? Take in every detail that you can of you and your horse's surroundings, and note all of your physical sensations as well. Feel your hands, your back, your feet on the surface that you are on. As you halter your horse, notice the way the air feels going in and out of your nostrils, and look closely at the tiny, soft hairs of your horse's muzzle, and their eyelashes. Allowing your focus to zoom in, as it were... to pay attention to just your breath, and just your horse's eyeball... this way of observing sometimes helps to dislodge our routine ways of thinking. If we honor and cherish the moments like these, with our horses, we can continue to return to them in this same, mystical way. Always practicing being grateful for moments like those, particularly while they are happening, is a great way to ensure their continuity.

Grooming

As you brush your horse, currying, mane combing, and hoof picking are some of the first places that we connect with a horse, once we bring the horse from their environment into our realm of direction. Of course, the main reason most of us groom our horses is to clean them to make sure they are comfortable when we ride them (and don't buck us off due to a burr...), but there are really many reasons to groom a horse.

Another reason is that we stimulate their surface dermal cells (skin), which actually increases circulation throughout the horse's entire body. One benefit that this has is that increased blood flow helps any physical ailments to heal more quickly. And also, that increase in circulation helps a horse's digestive processes work more efficiently and effectively. This means that grooming a horse can help reduce the likelihood of colic, how's that for a remarkable correlation?

Yet one more experience we can have while we are grooming a horse – if we are mindful enough – is to begin to actually become aware of the effects that occur as we enmesh the electromagnetic field that surrounds each of us with that of another lifeform's. This is actually far simpler to observe than it might sound. Before you begin brushing or massaging your horse, notice how you feel. Notice what thoughts you are having and what emotions you might be experiencing. Notice your horse, and notice what mood they may seem to be in - you may want to recall their demeanor which you observed earlier. Now notice your breathing and allow your mind to clear as you begin grooming your horse. As you do, continue working to keep your mind relaxed, and focused not on thinking, but on just being aware of experiencing your time with your horse. In the process of the exercise, notice if you don't find yourself and your horse getting to be almost in the same, if not similar, moods. This is the enmeshment I was referring to before. It is just simply what happens when you are in physical contact, paying attention to what is happening, and you don't allow yourself to be overwhelmed by your own thoughts. You can practice this with your dog or cat, or family member at home, and have the same results. But you must be diligent in your practice of quieting the mind and being mindful.

Now that your horse is all ready for some fun, try this simple pressure/release exercise:

Have your horse in a halter, not tied to anything. Grip the lead rope between your first finger and thumb. Apply constant, gentle pressure down until any downward movement of your horse's head occurs, and as soon as it does release all pressure. Continue this exercise (this may take days, weeks, or months – no need to rush) until the horse will maintain holding their head, for at least a short period of time, down somewhere near their knees.

I have a small collection of exercises which I will do regularly with horses in hand. You may want to incorporate some or all of these into your routine, or just be mindful in the groundwork exercises you already use.

Bending

First is Bending. I like to ask a horse to wrap its neck around me in order to get a bit of a stretch, and at the same time respond to a few familiar directives to get the connection started for the day's activities. Depending on the horse, I will either use their halter or a treat to encourage them to bend around me to both sides, and then stretch their nose down and back toward and between their knees.

Respecting Direction

It is handy for some horses to practice changing direction as they walk around you on the lead rope – this is a very good tool if your horse tries to dominate you as you work to send them out on the lunge circle. To practice Respecting Direction: as the horse moves around you in a circle on the lead rope, begin by holding the lead rope in one hand. Then lift the arm with which you are holding the lead rope straight out to your side. Then take your other arm and hold it directly out to your side, like the other one. Then you can move laterally – the direction your hand and arm are pointing, to the side – toward your horse's hindquarters, looking in that direction, not at your horse's face, and you can direct the front end of your horse with the lead rope while at the same time using your body, voice and gestures to propel your horse forward, primarily with the side of your body that is towards your horse's rump.

Once your horse is walking around you successfully in a circle, your hands and arms should return to what I call 'default': your upper arms should drop down from your shoulders by your sides or just in front of you; your lower arms from the elbows down are resting about horizontal, or level with the ground; and your hands can be pointed towards your horse, as though you were at the center of a pie-wedge, as described in lunging. If your horse is eager to respond to you, you can even drop your hands to your sides when you are not actively directing your horse. Particularly when you are teaching your horse something new, each time before asking them to do it again, or to do something different, allow your horse to do a few victory laps, and you may also want to praise them verbally to reaffirm to them that this is the desired objective.

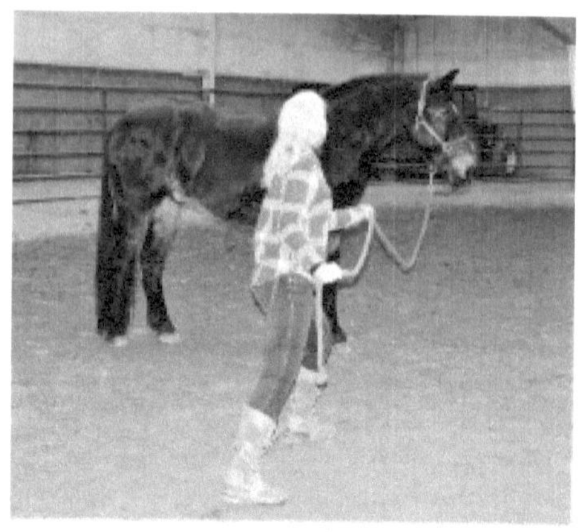

To change direction, you want to slow or stop your horse's progress by stepping laterally in front of their momentum (see Lunging for additional details). At the same time you step to be in front of your horse's forward motion, bring your hand which is holding the lead rope back toward your body. Then lean and reach forward with your other hand, and grab the lead rope at least two and a half feet up the lead rope from the end you are holding, and simultaneously step forward at an angle, toward the horse's head, so that you can see your horse's outside eye, while pulling your horse's head to the inside, by drawing your new leading hand back toward and even a bit behind your body, on the same side which that arm is on, which will make seeing that outside eye all the easier. Once your horse takes a step turning to go the other direction, move towards your horse, and then you repeat the actions that you used to send your horse out to circling around you in the first place.

Unwinding

Personally, my biggest challenge with the unwinding exercise is keeping track of which side I worked from last. The easiest way I've found for me – Miss Dyslexic – is to remember if I looked at the mane the last time or not. This, however, may be of little help when working with a very hairy horse. Begin by standing at your horse's shoulder facing your horse's tail. Place the lead rope over your horse's back with the end which is not attached to the halter over your horse's back on the opposite side from which you are standing. Next go to the other side. Take the lead rope and gently ease it over your horse's rump, but keep enough gentle tension on it that it does not fall below the point of your horse's hip – at least not while first practicing the exercise. Once the lead rope is positioned, stand back a few feet, and then without moving your feet, pull the lead rope and reel it in, gathering it up, until your horse bends their head away from you, follows with their hooves, and then comes all the way around to face you. Of course, don't get stepped on. As your horse learns this, you may need to protect yourself by stepping out of the way, but work to get them moving in a way that is considerate of you and your space. Repeat both directions multiple times. As you practice this exercise more, you may want to let the rope lay at many different heights around your horse's rear end, but don't let it fall below their hocks. Even at hock height, some horses panic and want to run away from that particular pressure, so be sure your horse feels safe with the rope higher up on their rump before proceeding to lower rope heights.

Lunging

In my training, I will use both a round pen and a lunge line for different types of work, and based on what is available in the horse's environment. In the Trustwork chapter later in this book, I will discuss a few practices for a round pen. And always remember, that if your horse is unfamiliar with lunging, a round pen is a great way to help them get comfortable with it – and help your shoulder to stay in socket as your horse learns.

If you are unfamiliar with it, lunging is the practice of sending a horse off in a circle around you, large enough for the horse to be able to canter, while you hold a rope in the middle of that circle. Doesn't that sound easy? It can be. In a nutshell: don't let the lunge line touch the ground, stay behind the horses heart, you may use a lunge whip to help your horse understand and propel it forward, and NEVER get distracted and caught up in the line – this is certain death. I am only kidding sort of.

The reason to use lunging in the pursuit of mastering Mindful Horseback Riding practices, is so you can see the horse moving at a good enough distance that you can easily see the entirety of the horse's body all at once. We can begin with a brief review of lunging and some pointers. Please, always wear gloves when you lunge any horse.

Using the lunge whip

Unless you have a very flighty horse, using a lunge whip in accompaniment to the lunge line is commonly a very effective method to encourage understanding of the lunging practice by the horse. If your horse is high strung they may try to run away when the lunge whip is present. If this is your circumstance, do not use a lunge whip, but if your horse needs more motivation than your hand alone, just make the lunge line a bit shorter, and hold the end of the line in your propulsion hand (see Lunging formation) to use in the same manner as the lunge whip – this will still be motivational, it will just not appear quite as threatening to your horse as the whip. Regarding use of the lunge whip specifically, remember there are several methods to use it, and none of the ones I am going to mention involve touching the horse. If your horse is more energetic, you can keep the rope-like part of the whip wrapped around the rigid part and even hold the very tip to secure it. That way, you only have a stick-like object pointed at them, rather than a snake-like item. My favorite way to use the lunge whip is with it unfolded and dragging on the ground. I do a lot of work with horses in fairly quiet settings, and it is quite handy to use the sound and rhythm of the whip dragging back and forth along the ground, perhaps in a circle, to be a constant motivator and reminder to the horse I'm working with of our connection. One can slap the ground with the lunge whip, in most any way that makes sense to you. Then for those horses that utterly lack drive, you can always crack the whip to make a loud reason for your horse to be propelled forward. Do this by raising the tip of whip off the ground, suspending it there for a moment, and then move the entire whip in a manner that sends the dangling tip straight in one direction, and abruptly yanks it back the opposite way. You may want to practice this without your horse if you want to feel confident at the time you are lunging.

Lunging Formation

Now let us look at the lunging formation. The formation you want to get to is that of a pie-wedge shape. Keep your shoulders square to your horse's spine. The horse should be a good distance away from you, at least 15 feet, and your hand that is holding the lunge line should be pointed at the horse's head. Your shoulder of that arm should be relaxed, the elbow slightly bent, and held at the height of your lower ribs, your wrist also relaxed. Your heart should be pretty much lined up when you are at rest, or in 'default' position, with your horse's heart, which is basically just behind their elbow. Your other hand, the one that is toward the tail of your horse, should be pointed right at or just behind your horse's tail, at basically the same height and in pretty much the same position as the other hand. Keep in mind it may be holding the whip or other end of the lunge line which is pointed at your horse's hindquarters. Yes, your arms and shoulders may get sore as you practice this, but don't worry, you are also building muscles, just like your horse.

From this position, if you step in front of your horse's heart, or towards their head, laterally, you will 'get in the way' of the horse's forward motion, and they will slow down or stop. If you step sideways towards your horse's tail, you will be getting out of their way, you will be encouraging their propulsion, and they will speed up. There's the basics of go and stop on a lunge line.

Speeding Up

A few more tips regarding propulsion include: if you have a very slow horse, you may need additional propulsion. That could include the lunge whip, and verbal cues like kissing, or clucking (one way to do this is you take your tongue, stick it to the roof of your mouth, and then pull it off quickly, making a popping sound), or other assorted sounds that might make a horse run from you if they were getting into mischief – like "ya!" or "git" or something similar. Another propulsion cue is stepping forcibly towards your horse's rump and stomping with your foot, which is closest to your horse's hindquarters, all in one motion. Always be consistent with your cues. Be sure that you have your shoulders back and your chest lifted, and that – particularly when you are propelling your horse forward – you are looking at your horse's hind end, not at their eye.

Slowing Down

A couple of tips regarding slowing down: use your voice here as well. A great tool to slow a horse down is to purr at them. You can do this by rolling your r's like you do in Spanish, (as in "perro") but without a word attached. Another example would be to purse your lips gently, and blow through them, letting them flap quickly as you force air through them. Always remember that when you want a horse to slow down while lunging, that you will want to take a step or two to get in the way of their forward momentum (see Trustwork).

Also, in your verbal tools, you can teach your horse that words like 'whoa' and 'ho' and 'easy' mean that they should slow down, or stop, simply by repeating those words to them as they do those things – but do keep in mind that teaching them those words is a far cry from shouting them at your horse in the hopes that they'll work. Also remember that if you do decide to teach your horse voice commands, pick one word for each action and dedicate that word to that action, so that you can be consistent. I will discuss this a bit more in the Trustwork section, but for instance, if you decide to use the command "Whoa!" to be the word which tells a horse to come to a complete halt, never use that word to tell a horse to slow down. If you teach a horse what a particular word means, only use that one word to describe that one action only. If you do not, chances are that your horse will not only get confused, but will likely learn to NOT trust you, because if they can't understand you, they won't be able to do what you ask, so you will likely always be confused or upset, which will be exactly your horse's experience as well. Be consistent – it makes for much happier equine encounters.

Turns

For turns, similarly to changing direction in Respecting Direction, step laterally towards the front of your horse, change hands with the lunge line, so that the line ends up in your hand that will be towards the head of your horse. Then reel the horse in a bit, or shorten the lunge line, so that the horse turns its head towards the inside of the circle, the one created going the direction you began with, enough so that you can see the eye that was away from you before. If you are using a whip, keep it low as you cross it under the lunge line to change hands with it also. Continue to look at that outside eye as you step toward that side of the horse and move the end of the whip or end of the lunge line or your hand towards the shoulder on the outside of the circle. Keep the line off the ground as the horse comes toward you and completes the half circle you were asking for, that change of direction. Try to make this as smooth and fluid an operation as you can. Practice repeatedly, every time you lunge, and remember always end any exercise on a positive note.

Come 'ere

One more tool for you and your horse is Come 'ere. If you teach this to your horse on the lunge line, it translates over to Trustwork well. This is a movement to finish with. Once your horse is stopped, and you are ready to change over to Trustwork or riding or putting your horse away, pat your chest a few times and say "Come 'ere" in an inviting voice to your horse. Then as soon as you have stopped patting your chest, reel your horse in with the lunge line, saying "Come 'ere" whole time, until you can reach out, touch your horse and give them some praise. Keep practicing this, and your horse will eventually learn it by voice command alone. You may even be able to teach your horse to do this particular activity when you go out to catch your horse. Just be patient, consistent, and keep working with it.

Starting the Lunge Circle

Where you look, in lunging and most aspects of horse work, can contribute greatly to how well your horse understands what you are asking. Many people will have trouble getting a horse to move away from them as they initially want to begin lunging. This can be a very effective way for a horse to passive aggressively resist your direction. Think how horses communicate with each other in the field. If they are not respecting you, you must strive to convince your horse that you are worthy of their respect. First, you must be sure that you are giving a completely clear signal.

Start by standing with your horse at a halt, facing your horse's barrel, behind their heart. When you first ask a horse to move out into the circle, look them in the eye, then look and step towards their hind end, though not into a position where you could be kicked, and raise your arm that is on the side of your body towards their hindquarters. If they then turn to face you, do not stare at them in the face, but look towards their flank, and move directly towards their hindquarters, in a straight line. And always remember: do not dance with the horse when you are lunging – save that for Trustwork. Lunging is an activity with purpose, direct and clear signals and outcomes. To the best of your ability, when lunging, keep your feet still – neither chase nor lead your horse where you want them to go. Direct them, clearly and concisely. And if you need to, always remember you can return to the Directing exercise done on a lead rope, which is described earlier in this Mindful Groundwork section.

Another reason one might use lunging as a tool is that as you move into Trustwork, you can use lunging to assist a resistant horse to regularly turn respectfully to the inside, instilling that habit in them so that when they do begin Trustwork, they are already used to turning to the inside.

Also, some horses want to hold their head to the outside, especially when they are working in a circle. This is not only bad for the horse physiologically, because a horse's muscles need to be aligned correctly in order to build properly, but it is also an indicator of disrespect, or at the least, disconnect, if there is a human at the center of that circle. Having a bit of pressure on the lunge line helps encourage a horse to have the right posture, for all the right reasons.

Alleviating Dizziness

One more suggestion to go with lunging, for those individuals prone to dizziness. Over my years of teaching these methods to hundreds of people, I have come across just a few techniques to avert or at least minimize the sensation of vertigo which can develop. First, there is a practice in dancing called spotting, which sometimes can help. To utilize this method in an equine setting, as your horse goes around their circle, find several stationary objects around the outside of that circle, or just beyond it. As your eyes follow your horse around, let them rest for about 10 to 15 feet of your horse's progress around the circle on 1 of those objects, then move your eyes over your horse and ahead of your horse to your next focal point. Let your eyes rest there until your horse has moved past your line of vision again, and then continue this practice. You can observe your horse when you are doing this by practicing with your peripheral vision. Some individuals also feel relief from dizziness by just walking and following their horse around in a tiny circle inside of their horse's circle, similar to the method used in Trustwork. And of course, much of the time, if you simply keep your horse far enough away and work at a walk or slow trot, your unpleasant experience may not occur at all.

Now with the basics of lunging in place, we can continue our journey through the human physiological and mental aspects of the Mindful Groundwork exercises which will lead us into Mindful Horseback Riding.

Breathing With Steps From A Distance

Ask your horse to walk out on a circle on the lunge line. Hold the lunge line long enough that you can easily see the movement of all four of your horse's hooves. Now as you watch each of the horse's hooves fall, begin to count the steps. It's generally easiest if you just focus on one set of hooves, the front or the rear. Begin by counting your horse's hoof steps - 1, 2, 3, 4, and repeat that, again and again. I suggest you start by counting out loud. And don't just count randomly. Pay close attention to the actual hoof falls of your horse, and count each time a hoof hits the ground. If they slow or speed up their cadence, let your count reflect that. After a little practice with this, if you have been counting out loud, you can begin counting to yourself, and start breathing in to a count of four of your horse's hoof falls, and out, to a count of four of your horse's hoof falls. Again, if your horse's cadence changes, allow your count and subsequent breath to be affected as well. Then you can allow yourself to continue counting, but let your count of the horse's hoof falls increase – just remember to always breathe out to the same count as you breathe in to. I personally like to get to 11 hoof falls each breath in, and each breath out. If you ever find yourself running out of breath before you run out of numbers, just exhale more slowly, particularly as you first begin to breathe out.

Remember that you should make this practice yours in whatever way feels right to you. You may want to count the rear hoof falls. You may want to count all four hoof falls, but remember if you do that, that you will likely count twice as high, as the beats will be happening twice as often. This exercise does not have to happen only at the walk. Just remember that in this situation, as the speed of the hoofbeats increases, the number of beats you count per breath must increase as well. You may notice that as you practice this each time, somewhere in the process, your horse finds a particular rhythm and stays there. This is an indicator of success – you have connected with your horse and the two of you are getting into sync. Another integral use of this particular breath practice is when you are working with leading horses, and this is a practice that we will also work with in mounted exercises. This is a great calming tool, whether mounted or on the ground, to help both horses and riders or handlers to relax.

Mindful Walking

This exercise translates into mounted activities as well, and this is generally some of the first homework that I send clients home with from Equine Assisted Therapy, to practice with their household pets. Begin walking with your horse. As you will remember from Mindful Groundwork, in the lunging section, we discussed noticing and counting your horse's hoof falls. As you walk with your horse, allow yourself to become aware of your horse's hoof falls in whatever way seems easiest for you. If you feel drawn to, look down at your horse's hooves as you walk beside them. Watch and count, and practice with this as long as you need, and you will eventually be able to become aware of and focus on those steps, even without looking at your horse's hooves. You may want to align your steps with your horse's steps, to bring you into even deeper connection – but that is not absolutely necessary. Just breathe in to a count of 4 of (you and/or) your horse's steps, and breathe out to 4 of those steps. Repeat this for a while, and then increase the number of steps you/your horse takes during the time it takes you to take a breath. Remember to keep your in breath and your out breath at the same number of counted steps.

As you feel successful with this exercise, you can begin to expand your experience of it. Play with breathing with different sets of hooves (try the rear if you're used to breathing with the front two hooves, or vice versa, or all four). As you work with this, take notice of your body. Lift your chin and bring your head back on top of your shoulders, not out in front of your body, and practice expanding your peripheral vision. Relax your jaw, your neck, and your armpits, and keep breathing. If you have another friend or family member who is a horse enthusiast like yourself, invite them to join you in this exercise. Explain it to them, help them, and then allow your awareness to encompass them as well as you and your horse. Maybe your partner walks on the opposite side of the horse from you, maybe they walk behind you with the rear set of hooves, if your horse is good with a person walking back there, or perhaps the other person walks by your horse's shoulder, as you walk by your horse's hindquarters. By doing this, you are not only sharing all this equine wonder and wellness with your friend, but you are also expanding your own experience of this practice as well.

Trustwork

Trustwork is a series of exercises which are done at least initially in a round pen, that were developed to put the human into the role of alpha within the herd which is created between horse and human. I won't go into herd hierarchy here, but the alpha is the leader of the herd. The alpha is constantly challenged to make sure they are always still good enough to lead the herd. The reason the human should be the alpha is so that they can remain safe, and so that the horse can be relaxed and attentive in their education, without having to worry about protecting the human. In this scenario, the horse gives their trust to the human. So do not despair if your horse continually pushes your buttons. They are just making sure you are still in this for the long haul. Just keep being consistent. You're telling them how much you love them and how trustworthy you are, by your actions.

I have mentioned voice commands earlier, in the lunging section. I feel that teaching a horse voice commands helps to give them one more way that they can understand what we are asking of them. The best way that I have found to teach any equine English, (or any language, for that matter) is to just simply tell them what they are doing, along with some sort of verbal praise, particularly when lunging or free lunging. So, if your horse is walking around, just tell them, "Good boy, good Bullet. Good walk, good boy. Good walk." Or "Good trot, Candy! Good girl, Candy, good trot!" When you talk to your horse you are establishing an invisible connection with your horse, and that can be a stronger tool than many people recognize. Also, always be consistent. Use the same word to describe the same action every time. As I have said before, do not use the word 'whoa' to describe both slowing down and stopping. Whatever words make sense for you, use, but make each word unique to each different action that you and your horse undertake.

Trustwork is a training tool as well, so if your horse does something like turn their head to the rail and their hindquarters towards you as they reverse, or anytime, except in Unwinding or similar exercises, you can let them know that was not the desired objective by making them canter around the round pen for at least 3 laps before you allow them to slow back down. Each time they behave similarly, behave similarly yourself. It is essential that you are consistent with your horse, using the same directions and the same responses every single time each action and interaction occurs. And if your horse has trouble with any of these progressive practices, just work on a slower or earlier exercise. For instance, if your horse is running amuck while trying to learn Trustwork, you could practice lunging for a longer period of time at higher speeds before switching to Trustwork, or you might let them canter without you directing them for a little while in the round pen before asking them to listen to you in Trustwork exercises.

Finally, Trustwork itself is an intricate methodology of developing the horse handler's role as herd alpha, which we are really just touching on here. These are some guidelines for this program. I encourage you to take what you can from these pages to develop your equine relationship in every way possible. And then... I am out here, I am slow to respond, but please feel free to reach out.

Go

The first step in Trustwork is Go. This is fairly simple. Ideally done without a lunge whip, but each horse and rider or handler pair is different. A lunge whip can be perfect in certain situations. Recall the pie-wedge shape from lunging. This will serve you in Trustwork as well. In Trustwork, you won't stand still in the center in the same way you do for lunging. In fact, although certain horses I have worked with are more than happy for you to stand motionless in the center of the round pen, giving only the tiniest cues for the horse to respond to, some horses will seem almost offended if you don't move around the round pen at least to some degree, with them.

In Trustwork, you might want to imagine that all of your movements have long extensions on them. For instance, you might imagine that your fingers have long ribbons on them, so long that when you wave your hand towards your horse, you actually brush their hindquarters with your ribbon-fingers. It may sound a bit silly, but you will see how handy this can be, if you try it with encouraging your horse, or getting your horse to turn.

Move your horse out towards the rail of the round pen. At this point, your horse can move at any speed. Once the horse is moving in one direction, do not allow them to change direction until you ask them to. Move in the round pen with them in a circle, slightly behind them, staying a safe distance away from their hindquarters, in a smaller circle than the circle which they are traveling around. If your horse tries to turn and go the other direction, move towards the edge of the round pen behind them and drive them, by means of your voice, waving your arms, and all other body language (and whip, if you are using one) to continue to keep them going in the same direction. If your horse dodges you and successfully goes the other direction, get in front of them –

maybe not directly in front of them, don't get run over and hurt, but be very clear that you are trying to impede their forward progress – and then drive them back in the direction they were initially going before they so abruptly tried to question your authority as alpha. Repeat this until your horse stops trying to go the other direction. And then... Turn.

Turn

Once your horse is agreeably Go-ing, you can ask them to Turn and change direction. This is a very calculated and mathematic equation that changes every time you do it, but once you and your horse get the hang of it, it is very simple to do, and appears remarkable to onlookers, as well. Imagine as you follow your horse around walking (or running) in your own circle, just a little behind and a good bit to the inside of them, that you could see the line you were creating in a circleas you went along. Now, as you walk this line, stop, and walk backward along this same line, this circle, pivoting, and keeping your shoulders square to your horse's spine. Continue through the apex of that circle, turning and beginning to walk forward and toward the rail, all the while still looking at your horse's head. You need to catch sight of your horse's outside eye, and then you might imagine that your fingers can actually stretch out and get between your horse and the rail, and just coax, or suggest that they turn their head towards you, and follow with their body to go the other direction.

If you are using a lunge whip, as soon as you stop and begin to go backward, drop the tip of the lunge whip to the ground, while you continue holding the handle. Drag it along the ground in an arcing and inviting circle, towards yourself, from their tail toward their head, and creating space in front of the horse, for them to step into, just as the path you are walking is doing. Change the hand you are holding the lunge whip in to the opposite hand, what will become the 'tail' hand, at the apex of your circle as you change direction. You may need to walk all the way to the rail, straight from the most distant point in your circle away from your horse, in order to get between your horse's outside eye and the rail, and then get them to turn towards you and head off in the other direction. Also, pause in your walking toward the rail if your horse puts their head up and turns away from you. Just take a few moments to allow your horse to bring their attention back to you and then proceed with the Turn.

If your horse refuses to turn toward you, practice with the same discipline I mentioned earlier, of driving the horse around without verbal praise for at least three laps before allowing them to slow back down. Then try the Turn with whichever direction they are going at the moment. All horses will favor one direction to turn over another. When the horse does Turn correctly, shower them in verbal praise and allow them to pause, or at the least not be directed at all, for a few moments as a reward, but gently encourage them onward if they try to stop or turn at all.

The idea with stopping and walking backwards is that your horse is paying attention to you. When you change what you have been doing and start to walk away from them, once you have established a good connection, they wonder what you are doing, and will often turn just at that point to see what you are doing. At which point you head toward the rail in front of them without walking directly at them, and encourage them to continue coming toward you and then moving away from you as they finish their change of direction by heading off in the new direction, moving back out onto the rail. We always want a horse to turn towards us because this shows that the horse respects us. When a horse turns their hind end towards us, in this exercise, it tells us that the horse does not trust us, feels unsafe, or does not respect us for any possible collection of reasons. This is the horse saying "I will kick you if you push too hard", which is why we work with the horse until its behavior indicates that it has put us in charge, and is willing to humor us and listen to what we have to say, at least for a while.

Stop

Depending on the horse, some will respond to Turn more readily, and some will be more receptive to Stop. Now is the time to learn which is easier for your horse to wrap his or her mind around. Stop will, like much of Trustwork, most likely require some finessing to find the exact equation which works best for you and your horse. Remember, that much of working with horses is translation: what you are trying to direct the horse to do, to the horse; and what is making the horse resist your direction, to you.

Stop is very similar in its cue to Turn. The first thing you do in cuing a horse to Stop is to do just that, stop. Drop the tip of the lunge whip, if you are using one, to the ground or, depending on your horse, you may want to drop the whip to the ground completely. If your horse has not already stopped with this body language, I use that purring sound, mentioned in the Lunging section earlier in this chapter, immediately followed by "Whoa!", the combination of which is my dead-stop verbal command, and take a step or two laterally toward the horse's head. This will get in the way of their forward momentum. If at this point your horse begins to run to make it through the shrinking window that is before them, back up to where you are in a position by the rail a good distance along the round pen in front of your horse, or step to just behind your horse as they come past you, so that when they come around again on the next lap, they can see you coming for a good ways. If you have any concern for your safety at this point, return to lunging and practice Stop in lunging until your horse is more receptive to it. If you can tell your horse is just being silly or harmlessly belligerent, and you feel safe in proceeding, stand with your arms at about waist or chest high, with the hand that would have been pointed toward your horse's head closer to the rail. You want to try to achieve a soft bend in your body, from one hand to the other, as though if you were a wall, you would turn your horse off of the rail and send them in toward the middle of the arena. If any of these methods are successful in getting your horse to come off the rail of the round pen with their head turning towards you, immediately follow their tails and push them out into going along next to the rail in the opposite direction. And then Pause, but as you Pause in this situation, continue moving, just not directing. If you stop completely, it is likely your horse will consider this a direction, and cease their progress along the rail entirely.

If your horse is consistently resistant to Stop or Turn, you can help them through some of the insecurities they may be experiencing by working them through the same exercises on the lunge line. Be sure to use the same body language with lunging as you would in Trustwork. Remember with a lunge line, always make sure you keep the lunge line up off the ground, so that your horse cannot step over it and put themselves into a position where they could give themselves a rope burn.

Connecting

Once you have an understanding with your horse regarding how Trustwork works, practice your exercises of counting steps here as well. Once all this connecting happens, your horse is likely to be so filled with gratitude for the connection that you two have developed and all the time you're spending together, that they will want to Connect with you. See if your horse is ready for this by going and standing by your horse's head, facing the same direction your horse is facing, at a standstill. Give a quiet kiss sound, look at your horse in the eye, look back ahead and slowly begin to walk forward, without looking back at your horse to see if they're coming. Once your horse is Connected, you can practice walking and turning and even running around with your horse. This gives you both confidence, and builds and strengthens the bond between the two of you.

Earlier, in the lunging section, I mentioned that we should save the dancing for Trustwork. Using all of the techniques you have learned thus far, you and your horse can create beautiful, elegant, joyful experiences. If you want, you can play music during this, which many times bystanders appreciate as well. Some movements you could choose to use might include: connecting Turns 180 degrees across the round pen repeatedly;

transitioning from trot to canter every few steps; halting from a higher speed; and of course, Connecting.

More Advanced

A slightly more advanced movement is the Two Form Pirouette. To execute this movement, first Connect with your horse, and walk. Make an ever-tightening circle with your horse, with you on the inside of the circle. When you get to the point that your circle is so small you are basically spinning in place, and your horse is walking around the outside of you, begin to spin the other way, while continuing to encourage your horse to keep going the way they are moving. Do a few spins like this (but don't get dizzy and fall over!) Be aware when your horse's head is right next to you and depart the circle fluidly, catching your horse intentionally and taking them with you back out in a new direction. Once horses get the hang of this, most of them are just as eager to play in this way as in any other.

You can use Trustwork to help quiet your mind in yet another way. As you work with Trustwork, you can begin to see how you are watching the horse to give you very subtle clues as to what they are thinking, and what they might be planning to do next. Always watch to see if your horse is doing the same thing, or something very similar, in the same spot each time they go around the round pen. This could indicate a distraction to the horse, like 'oh, my friends are over there', or 'here's the gate, can I leave yet?' And if you continue to pay attention, you will begin to notice that you miss certain subtleties which your horse is offering you, if you are off in your own thoughts. Allow this knowledge to be to your benefit. Allow yourself to just gently brush aside the thoughts you notice coming into your mind which do not relate to the present moment with what is going on with the horse you are with right now. Breathe and concentrate, but let your mind relax, also. Just be here with your horse in this moment.

IV. Mindful Horseback Riding

As you prepare to mount your faithful steed, just remember that you only get one brain, and no matter how mindful you are, accidents do happen. It is always wise to wear a helmet while riding.

Dismounted Stretches

All of these exercises work with any tack, or no tack at all. Attire yourself and your horse to be comfortable, safe, and balanced. Let us begin with a few exercises. It is always advisable to stretch and warm up before any physical activity, and horseback riding is no exception.

Begin with horse stance, feet wide apart, knees over toes, shoulders over hips, hands together and hold for 20-30 seconds. Follow that with a few lunges against your horse's shoulder or barrel, be sure to do both legs, holding as you stretch each leg for 10-30 seconds. Bend over and touch your toes, or as close as you can get, and hold for 10 seconds. Now mount up, as the rest of the stretches are done on your horse!

These exercises are designed for a horse that does not run off the moment you drop the reins. If you have a horse that is a bit more inclined towards motion, you may want to ask someone to help you stay safe the first few times your get familiar with the exercises. If you do these exercises in tack, I suggest you keep your feet in the stirrups as you learn them.

Yoga on Horseback

Around 2006 I created a program of Yoga on Horseback which I taught a lot, in private and group sessions. In following years we worked on several projects, including a Yoga on Horseback calendar and demonstrations across the nation. The fundamentals of Yoga on Horseback are as much a part of Mindful Horseback Riding as anything I teach. An aspect of yoga is combining breathwork with movements. These practices bring you into the present moment, focusing you on your breath and connecting you with your horse ever more deeply, the more you practice.

Basic Position

Begin by sitting on your horse in a balanced and comfortable position. First, if you don't know where your sitz bones are, find them. They are the raised bumps on the lower back portion of the three fused bones that make up the pelvis. Locate them on your body by putting your fingers or hands under your buttocks, palms up, from behind as you are sitting on your horse. They are the pointiest bones you find, one on each side. Now, open your pelvis. Do this by turning your attention to one leg at a time, and only for the sake of description, let's start with the left leg. Reach down with your left hand, palm facing your leg, and place the fingers of your left hand at least half way, if not more, under the back of your thigh, about two-thirds of the way up your leg from your knee. This will be about 6 to 8 inches straight down the underside of your thigh from your sitz bone, or about half way under your leg. You may want to put your fingers under your leg with your thumb on top. Then take your right hand and place it directly across your left thigh from your other hand, as though you were strangling your leg. Now, lift your leg just a bit, with your hands, not so much with your leg, and rotate your leg so that the fingers of your right hand turn their tips down towards your horse and under your leg, and the fingers of your left hand pull up, turning the underside of the back of your leg up, back and out. Now repeat with the other side. If you have ever noticed your stirrups seeming not the same length as usual, try this technique and see if it affects your experience. What happens is that as you take the seated position, you jam the ball of your hip into the back of its socket. When you do what I describe here, you are simply allowing that joint more mobility so that you can have a better, more fluid, and flexible experience as you ride.

Now that your pelvis is open, elongate. Remember to keep breathing, continue letting your thoughts go, and just keep returning to the present moment. Imagine that you have four coins about the size of quarters on the bottoms of each of your feet, bottoms of each of your feet, 2 on either side of the bottom of your heels, and 2 on either side of the balls of your feet, about an inch to an inch and a half towards the arch of your foot, down from your toes. Become very aware of these coins. Stretch all four of them on both feet down toward the earth, simultaneously. Notice your heels stretching down with just as much attention as you notice of the balls of your feet stretching down. And as you notice your lower extremities in this way, just begin to direct your attention to your pelvis, your hips, your waist and your spine. If you like, you can place your hands on your upper thighs, and push your upper body away from your lower body, or just let them rest on the reins or the withers. Imagine, that each of your vertebrae is separating just a tiny bit from the one next to it, as are your ribs, as your whole ribcage lifts up, from your lowest ribs. Feel the vertebrae in your neck as well, and then just allow your skull to come back into a natural alignment by bringing your head back over your spine, as though you were lifting gently up and back from just below your ears. Keep your shoulders and jaw relaxed as you do this.

This is your basic position. After you do each stretch, return to this position: your feet stretched down, mostly from your heels, but from all quadrants of your feet, and your entire torso lifted up and back from just below your ears. Remember that you want to be elongated and engaged, but not rigid or inflexible. These movements help to isolate different ways you move on a horse, stretch pertinent muscles, and prepare you for the psychophysiological interactions to follow.

In general, as you lengthen your muscles or stretch out your body, be conscious of breathing in, and as you contract your muscles or fold your body, be aware of breathing out. I am not saying only breathe in as you stretch and out as you contract, at least not initially. Be very aware of a long, deep in breaths during stretches, and long, deep out breaths as you bend.

Arms Shoulder Height

Look forward. Raise your arms to shoulder height, out from your body to the sides. At the same time that you are aware of stretching up and down, stretch your fingertips out to your sides. Be aware of your shoulder blades coming together, and your breastbone feeling as though it is elongating and lifting. Let your shoulders drop away from your ears. Hold this for 10 to 30 seconds, and then turn your body so that one of your hands points toward your horse's ears, and your other hand points toward your horse's tail. Keep your arms at shoulder height, and let your head turn comfortably to point in the direction your shoulders are facing. Breathe deeply, slowly, and regularly. Hold this for 5 to 20 seconds and then turn to the other side, noting all the same details, and hold for the same amount of time as you held when you were facing the opposite direction.

Repeat if desired.

Bends and Turns

With your arms still raised – or drop them for a moment if they feel tired, then lift them again – turn and point one hand towards your horse's tail and one toward your horse's ears. Take a deep breath in and then bend forward as you exhale, reaching as though you were trying to touch your horse's ears, while you stretch your other arm which had been pointed at your horse's tail straight out behind you. Stretch in this position for 5 to 20 seconds, breathing slowly and deliberately. Then come to an upright position again, turn the other way, and repeat the same stretch, including the deep breath, and exhale before you bend over. When you come up, drop your arms, turn 180 degrees again, and look back toward your horse's tail. Then stretch back, sliding your hand down your horse's back, over their hindquarters, over their dock, and to the top of their tail. This time you can let your other hand rest on your saddle or your horse's mane or withers to keep yourself balanced. You can stretch here for about 5 to 10 seconds. Come back up, change the direction you face and repeat the exercise on the other side. Then rest for a moment.

Chest Opening

In this next exercise, depending on your balance and your tack, you may want to bring your feet back up behind you, so that your heels almost run into your legs, or even come a little bit back up behind you, onto the back of your horse. If this doesn't work for your lower body, just keep your heels down and concentrate on pulling your heels back toward your horse's hocks. Place your hands comfortably behind you with your fingers pointed back toward your body. Begin to tilt your head back as you bring your shoulder blades together, it should feel as though you are trying to open your chest up towards the sky, and the rest of your body is stretching back from the center of your chest. Do this stretch for 10 to 30 seconds, then slowly relax and come back to a resting position.

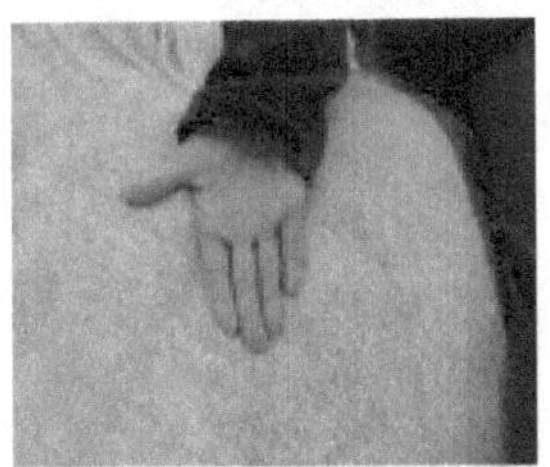

Triangle

Begin this last stretch by putting the back of your right hand across your horse's neck and flat against your horse's left shoulder. Move your right hand straight down towards the ground as you twist your body and bring your left arm straight up in the air above you. Continue to stretch down until, ideally, your shoulder blade is near your horse's withers, and your legs and feet are positioned straight down from your hips, without squeezing your horse's sides enough to make the horse walk off. Hold this for 10 to 20 seconds, and then slowly come back up and repeat on the other side.

By this point, you should be feeling very relaxed, connected with your horse, peaceful, and perhaps even at one with your surroundings. Most of these exercises can be done in motion as well as while standing, so feel free to integrate them into your riding routine in whatever way inspires you.

Mounted Walking Meditation

I recommend initially learning these exercises in a round pen or an arena, solely so that you will be less likely to be interrupted by a stumble or other unexpected change in the environment, as one might find out on a trail. But like with most things mindful, as you become familiar with them, they will become easy to practice in all kinds of circumstances and terrains, whether in company or alone.

Begin at a walk. Start to allow yourself to find the hoof beats in a similar but new way. Perhaps you may first notice your horse's front hooves, then you might see if you can differentiate the rear hooves from the front hooves. Then you might notice if you can isolate and identify all four hoof beats, independently. When you find the rhythm that you like the best, breathe in to a count of four hoof beats, and breathe out to a count of four hoof beats. Then allow yourself to slowly increase your hoof beat count to a rhythm that feels good and maintainable for you. Then just breathe at that rhythm for a while. This should be comfortable, in and out to the same number hoof beats. Perhaps find the maximum you can maintain comfortably, and then back off 1 or 2 hoof beats from your maximum.

Notice as you practice this how much clearer everything may appear to you, visually. You may even notice how you can possibly imagine that your mind feels a little more like your horse's mind... and that is because you are using this vast mind we humans have to be able to connect to and experience reality in a manner much more like the way your horse normally experiences it. When you clear away your extra thoughts, and are just present, this big ole mind of ours will focus on that which is around us. In doing so, we actually do perceive more colors, we may feel that we experience crisper or clearer vision – it's not so much a mystery as it is science. When the mind is focused and undistracted, it views more clearly, more completely, more effectively and efficiently. All of the body actually works like that...the less clogged it is with preoccupation, toxins or trauma, the better each of the body systems work, in humans and animals alike.

Circle

Now that you feel so connected in this way, begin to notice your body as you ask it to interact with your horse by riding through a circle. As you start to think about the circle you are about to make, notice your eyes as you begin to look to the inside of the arena or round pen, and as you lean just a tiny bit to the inside of where the circle will be, notice your outside leg and how you turn your toe a small amount in, toward your horse's side. Notice how your knee, on what will be the outside of the circle, shifts just a tad, too. Then how as you put just a little weight on your inside leg, how your hip and pelvis drop just a hair to what will become the inside of your circle as well. Become aware of how, as you have looked to the inside of your circle, you are actually in your peripheral vision seeing your horse's head, and by now your horse may have begun to turn a little as well. You may realize that you are actually looking down, just a bit. So you look up, and as you do so, you sit back, just a touch. And as you do so, your body settles onto your horse's back differently, and your inside shoulder drops, and your inside hand comes back almost imperceptibly towards your hip on that side. Your horse's turn becomes an actual circle, rather than just coming off the rail a tiny amount, or just a slight adjustment to your trajectory. Complete your circle being aware in this manner, entirely present with every action that you are making, and as you finish your circle, straighten back out and feel every movement that is a part of that. As you practice in this way, strive to be this aware of how you experience all of your movements, and maintain your breathing, in and out to the same number of steps continuously, all at the same time.

A few words about thinking about two things at once, while working to be mindful. The way I do this is to take the basic element and embed it into my lower thinking, which I perceive when thinking about it as under my eyes, under my view, or in my body. Then I use my regular view to address that which I perceive as more complicated, in this case spreading my awareness to be able to notice and distinguish all the different movements that are happening as I ride. You might compare this to ballroom dancing or ballet: The "one-two-three" or "one-two-three-four" rhythm present in classical dance, is known as the count. As you begin to learn, you embed that count into your mind as you then learn all the steps to all the different dances that go with that count. Eventually, you dance and dance, and that count is always present and underlying all of the movements, yet beneath them, not obscuring in any way, only informing and creating a platform upon which to build.

Figure Eight

Once you have become very comfortable with this Mindful Horseback Riding practice of a circle, extend this work into a figure eight. Horses are creatures that like patterns, which means that most of them, most of the time, like to find a rhythm, get into it, and stay there with minimal encouragement for a fairly lengthy period of time, depending on their age and stamina. When you practice a figure eight, it lets you stay in the rhythm of a pattern while still getting to practice the exercise in both directions, which is essential for staying in balance. You may want to practice your figure eight as though it was two circles which you connect in the middle. An integral part of this exercise is the way you pay attention to changing your balance in the center, between the two circles.

As you come back towards the center of your figure eight, completing one circle and about to begin the next, notice how much of your body is shifted toward the center of the circle which you are just finishing. Breathe in deeply and fully, and allow yourself to begin to straighten back up, mainly by noticing the quadrants of your feet and stretching them back down, toward the ground, and by lifting your upper body and thinking about bringing your head back and up, from just below your ears. Do this subtly and slowly, so that you are centered only just as you are about to go the other direction, as you cross over your own tracks to start the other half of your figure eight. Then as you look the other direction and start to be aware of beginning that whole process of being present through turning to the other direction, exhale slowly and fully. Continue to practice this until your feel fluid and you are able to make figure eights consistently.

Transitions

Transitions are a challenge at any speed, so beginning to practice them at the slowest speeds first makes sense. This is a truth that you can apply to everything you do with a horse, so always try to remember: if you find yourself struggling with almost any exercise with your horse – slow it down, and try it when the speed and vibration aren't so high. If you can't do that, then slow your vibration down – by using your breath, meditation, Chi Gong, or whatever works best for you, to calm yourself down. Just slow down, breathe deeply, and then you will be able to see better. This will allow you to find the solution more effectively. Especially for transitions, keep the idea in mind that your objective is to make all of your communications to your horse – eventually, at least – so subtle that no one watching could perceive them at all.

Begin from a halt. Balance yourself, and stretch down into all four quadrants of your feet, allow your chest and ribcage to float up and gently out in front of you, as you bring your ears back, until your shoulders are over your hips, and you level your chin. As you cue your horse to walk, pay close attention to your body. You want to be able to incline forward almost imperceivably with just your ribcage and upper body for only the instance in which your horse begins to step off into the walk. Settle your ribcage immediately back into its lifted but resting position below your shoulders, which are riding right over your hips. To be able to do this requires a great deal of perception and communication, both of which you will continue to build with your horse through many of the practices in this program. Coming back to a halt from the walk is not difficult, but when perfected, it is all you need in a day to be happy. All you have to do is lean back just a touch, with enough tension in your stomach and back muscles that you don't fall forward as your horse comes to a halt. You can push your heels out in front of you just a tiny bit to absorb the cessation of motion. Most of all, keep your pelvis grounded, and lift up from your waist as you stretch down into your feet. Practicing and refining your intricate understanding of the details which orchestrate these movements will allow you to be able to translate that into a seamless experience of all transitions in both directions – which is truly a great ability to have in one's repertoire. This is a testament to one's balance, and one of the best ways I know to stay safe is to understand the undertaking, whatever the task at hand may be.

By this time, you are most likely getting a pretty good idea of what Mindful Horseback Riding is and how it works. The biggest part is that you are present with your horse. That means that you are right there with your horse, noticing his respirations, not thinking about tonight's football game. You are seeing the eyelashes on her inside eye, coming through the turn, rather than eyeing that handsome cowboy, or pretty equestrienne sitting at a picnic table across the way. You are feeling the rhythm of your horse's hoof falls, as opposed to feeling the grumbling of your hungry stomach. On that note, whenever possible, stay nourished and hydrated when you work with horses. Being hungry, thirsty, or over tired are very common reasons to feel like you are not having success. Any compromised condition can lead to making a decision that may not be the best. Always take care of yourself, so that you can stay safe, take care of your horse, and thoroughly enjoy your time with your horse.

Higher Ground

Now that you are well on the way to mastering the aspects of Mindful Horseback Riding from the ground up, next I will discuss some exercises to deepen your connections with your equine partner even further.

As you prepare to come up into a trot, a jog, or whatever the next highest speed is for your horse, let your horse have a bit of forewarning in one or more of any number of ways. You can adjust your reins, if you are using them. With English reins you traditionally will shorten them just a hair, to give the horse what is known as 'a little more contact'. You may want to lean forward a touch, so that you tip forward off of your sitz bones for a moment before rocking back onto them in a cue of propulsion. Or you may just want to stretch down into your heels and wrap your legs around your horse and use that as a slow introduction to an ever tightening pressure that will elevate your horse into the next gait up.

I discussed some aspects of propulsion in both the lunging and Trustwork sections, so let us now address forward motion under saddle (or under rider, as the case may be). A rider can use their lower body to urge a horse forward. This can mean squeezing with the thighs, calves, buttocks, knees, ankles or feet, or any combination thereof. It can also mean kicking with the heels against the horse's sides, preferably in the general vicinity of the horse's girth, not farther back, as riders are sometimes inclined to do. It is ideal to kick with your heels down, in order to engage more muscles and bring more surfaces of the leg into contact with the horse. Keeping your heels down as you kick will also help your feet to come into contact with your horse near the girth, and help to keep you in better balance, by engaging the muscles on the undersides of your legs, which is where you should most sensibly grip your horse from anyway. Using your seat to follow the motion of your horse, and then overexaggerating that motion, can often encourage a horse to pick up its pace, as well. This following with your seat is described more completely in the section on sitting the trot. And of course, you can always use your voice to make encouraging sounds like clucking or kissing, and once your horse completely understands voice commands, then those will become part of your toolbox as well. Always be certain that you are not sending mixed signals like holding the reins too tight while asking the horse to move forward.

Remember from transitions, that you want to be so still that no one watching can perceive that you are telling your horse to do anything at all. You want it to appear as though you think it and the horse does it. Which is almost exactly what really does happen. Prepare by stretching your lower body down into your heels, and lifting your upper body up from your lowest ribs. Allow yourself to imagine spreading your awareness not only throughout your whole body, but letting that awareness include your horse, entirely, and the surface your horse is traveling on, and the surrounding environment as much and as far as you are able to. As you do this, be aware of making the movements in your body occur just as you want them to, just as they are described here, just as you know they do from the times you have done this successfully in the past. Then come up to the next gait faster, while being aware of every motion, every muscle, every thought that it takes to get there.

Sitting Trot

I feel it is important to be able to be mindful through all aspects of riding, and at this point I would like to discuss sitting the trot. One of the most important aspects of being able to comfortably sit the trot is being able to make sure your horse is moving at the right speed. Posting to the trot, or rising, is used when your horse is going along at a good clip. Posting occurs naturally, as the bounce of the gait actually throws the rider up off of the horse's back, to a small degree, and then they set themselves back down, poised in preparation of the next step. When a rider sits the trot, the horse needs to be going slower in their diagonal progressive speed - a jog or collected trot is the speed a horse is should be moving in order for the rider to be capable of sitting it. When moving at the walk, notice your vertebrae between your waist and your tailbone. Somewhere in there, probably about two to four inches below your waist, as you pay close attention, you will notice a little flexion there, a little squish, squish, squish as you feel those vertebrae flexing just a tiny bit so that your seat doesn't slap on the saddle, and your head doesn't swing too hard forward and back. That little squish between your vertebrae that you felt at the walk, and your initial over exaggeration thereof, is your key to a much more comfortable experience of the sitting trot. And remember: always strive to be mindful and present, through all of these exercises. Being focused and undistracted while working with thousand pound animals never did anyone a disservice.

Many times, at any gait, the rider, for any number of reasons, including but not limited to concentrating too hard, may develop what is known as a stitch in their side – a sharp pain which is normally near the lower ribs, which usually really is due to having actually forgotten to breathe. The walking meditation I described earlier works exceptionally well for helping to resolve that particular self-induced ailment, and you can utilize it at the trot as well. And remember from the earlier groundwork section, that breathing with the hoofbeats can be used to calm a horse – even more effectively while you are on their back.

Posting Trot

And here are just a few words about posting the trot. First, I highly recommend practicing posting bareback or without stirrups, and then translating that experience of your posting back over to when you are in the saddle. When you rise out of the saddle, try not to come up too far, ideally not more than an inch. This takes more effort to learn, but the rewards are great once your muscles get used to it. As you sit back down, use your inner thigh muscles, your mid back muscles, and the muscles behind your knees to set yourself gently down on your horse's back, in preparation for the next step to lift you up off of your horse's back again. Work to keep your feet back under your hips, while you bring your shoulders back, and as you hold your stomach in. If you are not certain of your success, try having someone take a short video of you. Compare what you see to what you seem to be feeling, and adjust accordingly. The physical dynamic this creates strengthens your core and keeps you in a position of control. Be sure to keep your hands low, down by your horse's neck, so that your movements do not distract your horse from its forward motion.

As you work with the trot, expand your exercises. Add squares and serpentines and trotting over poles to your exercises, and of course practice these at the walk, as well. Notice your body as you practice. Where are you looking? Are you elongated in your posture? Notice your mind – has it begun to wander, or are you still being attentive to the present moment? Feel how as your horse moves over poles, their motion changes. Do you stare at the poles as you go over them, or are you using your peripheral vision to hold them in your awareness? Notice how your horse turns to look around a corner, just as you turn your head.

One more workout for the posting trot, and this time I mean an even more exerting physical exercise than your average ride. Here is a very simple route to six-pack abs. You might take a picture of your body in the mirror before you begin. You can even hold your stomach in if you want to. At least 3 days a week, ride your horse. During your rides, hold in your stomach and lowest abdominals, without cessation, at the posting trot, for at least three minutes consecutively, at least three times during each ride, a minimum of three days a week. Do not forget to breathe while doing this exercise. After six weeks of doing this dedicatedly, hold your tummy in and look at your body in the mirror, maybe take another picture to compare to the first one. If you like the changes you see, just keep it up, and enjoy your extra reasons for spending time with your horse.

Cantering or Loping

Cantering or loping is mechanically easiest for a horse to go into from the walk, and although normally we first are introduced to this gait by running into it from the trot or jog, it is good to practice all the different transitions to and from all the different gaits. Remember that while the motion of the trot is vertical in nature, the canter is a round motion, that starts as your seat hits the back of your saddle at the moment your horse's initial single rear hoof hits the ground. You sink down into the saddle as your horse's diagonal hooves strike the earth, and you slide forward to the front of your saddle as those hooves pull your horse forward. As the last forehoof touches down, and in the moment of suspension when the horse has all four feet off of the ground, the top of the circular motion occurs in which the rider comes up off of the front of the seat of their saddle, and then experiences their own moment of suspension and then their seat comes back down onto the rear of the saddle, and then it all happens again.

Cantering or loping brings with it the fun and expansive opportunity to practice counting strides. This activity is wonderful when combined with mindfulness to bring confidence and peace to a gait which we commonly consider to be incredibly invigorating and exciting, and which many people only experience for very short periods of time. This exercise can help some riders to become confident in ways which enables them to enjoy the lope or canter for more extended periods of time. Counting strides is like counting hoof falls, except since the speed is so much faster overall, we count the entire stride as our connection, while we are aware of the three beats of the gait within in each stride. Those 3 beats are the moment the first hoof strikes the ground, as the 2 diagonal hooves hit the ground simultaneously, and as the final hoof lands before the moment of suspension as it all starts over.

Here are some ways to practice counting strides. Make sure to allow yourself to remain aware of the circular motion of the gait throughout these exercises. Practice breathing in to a comfortable count of strides, and out to that same count of strides. Then, count strides along the sides of the arena you ride in. Next, do not include the corners of the arena, just count when your horse is on a straightaway. Start with the long sides of the arena. Each side you go down, count; one, two, three...etc. A horse's stride is anywhere between 10 and 12 feet, depending on the size of your horse, so if your arena is, for instance, 100 feet long, if you take out room for the corner, you will likely only get 5 to 7 strides, even on the long sides, so do not expect your counts to be very high. If you do not have an arena and you are riding in a field or pasture, you may want to set some cones, or logs, or pile up some rocks at the corners of an imaginary arena space, and then work within its imagined confines. If you like, you can practice with this until you can count strides as you breathe your breath in during your traverse down one long side of the arena, hold your breath for the short side, exhale for the same count of strides along the other long side, hold the exhale on the other short side, then begin again with the first long side.

Be careful with this practice – know from all your earlier practice at lower speeds what your breathing limits are, what they feel like in any circumstance. Working at higher speeds is more exerting and more depleting than working at slower speeds, and if you have a larger arena, you may want to make a smaller square or rectangle within that entire work space, perhaps even creating physical boundaries by laying some poles on the ground. If you push too hard with this particular practice, you will end up on the ground, but don't let that scare you off from trying! Just let this be an exercise you approach with a not only good deal of respect, but also let all of your practice up to this point inform you about your own unique experience and understanding of this work and your own physical parameters.

Getting Perspective

Another exercise for working with counting strides is simply by laying poles on the ground and cantering or loping between them. There are distances that poles should be apart for each speed: 2 ½ to 3 feet for walk poles; 4 to 4 ½ feet for trot poles, and; 9 to 10 feet apart for canter poles. If you have never done any work with poles, it is a very good idea to practice with the ideal spacings before working as I am going to suggest later, as that will help your horse to build strength and balance in ways that will build muscles and coordination in the all right places.

You can begin to practice going over groupings of 2 to 6 poles in a straight line at the walk, trot and canter. Start in a straight line at least 35 feet in front of the poles, and notice how each time, as your horse approaches the poles, that they have to have their feet positioned in the proper way in order to enter into the string of poles and not hit every single one. Keep noticing how, during this approach to the poles, you can begin to see how your horse needs to either lengthen or shorten their strides, from farther and farther away as you approach the poles. Begin to help your horse by slowing them down or speeding them up a good ways off, so that they can step into the poles just right, without having to adjust their stride at all once they get there.

When you spend progressively more time on this exercise, you can begin to arbitrarily place poles around, and practice randomly walking, trotting, and cantering between these poles, turning at different places each time, practicing being able to see your horse's stride countdown to the poles more clearly each time. And as you get continually more comfortable using all of your Mindful Horseback Riding practices to work in unison with your equine partner, you become ever more capable of sharing every motion, vibration and veritable thought with your horse. You can utilize all of these exercises to build an ever strengthening line of communication and respect between you and not only your horse and the other horses you ride, but all of the horses that you come into contact with.

As you work at higher speeds particularly, always remember that consistency, patterns, and pauses continue to be integral tools to help you and your horse find your way along a mindful path. Remember that your balance and fluidity affects not only your comfort, but the comfort of your horse, as well.

V. Conclusion

I have put together this compilation of concepts, methods and practices with the intention that readers will be able to gain some insight into how they can be a better team member with their equine partners. Horse people who have worked with me in person recognize many of these practices and have appreciated that the techniques have been placed into an organized format so that they can refer back at any time if they should have questions. I have strived to be as clear and concise as possible, and have written in a conversational tone, in the hopes that these ideas will be easily understood. It is my desire that you will be able to use these pages to serve you well.

Over the course of the next several months, or even several years, that you work with the ideas inscribed on these pages, may you have success instilling these concepts so deeply and comfortably in your psyche that they truly become a second nature for you. So practice, and keep your eyes open. I have more to share with you on the topic of Mindful Horseback Riding, but I wanted readers to have the opportunity to take in all of these basic concepts and have time to work with, process, and assimilate them, without rushing into more advanced activities too quickly. This is all about Mindfulness, so I want to help you to take your time. There will be an advanced installment to follow which will bring you even closer to your horse by building on these fundamental lessons.

www.ingramcontent.com/pod-product-compliance
Lightning Source LLC
Chambersburg PA
CBHW031437130726
47989CB00003B/1181